HANDCRAFTING A GRAPHITE FLY ROD

L. A. GARCIA

COVER & ROD BUILDING PHOTOGRAPHS BY TONY OSWALD

GUIDO RAHR III

Frank Amato

PORTLAND

ACKNOWLEDGMENTS

I wish to acknowledge Mr. Willis G. "Bill" Chaplin Jr. of Raytown, Missouri who taught me my first skills as a rod builder. The year was 1974. Not only was he a skilled rod builder and fly fisherman but a gentleman in every sense of the word. He passed away in a tragic automobile accident on 22 May 1984.

I want to thank Tom Dorsey, Oren Clark, Tom Moran and the staff of Thomas & Thomas. Thomas & Thomas provided the blank used in the photographic sequences for the preparation of this book. Most of the information in Chapter 16 was provided by the staff of Thomas & Thomas. The information contained therein is included with the full knowledge and consent of Thomas & Thomas and in no way compromises information they consider proprietary.

Muchas gracias para mi buen amigo Bruce Staples of Idaho Falls, Idaho and author of Snake River Country Flies and Waters. It was Bruce who encouraged me to contact Frank Amato about a book on rod building.

Muchas gracias to Frank Amato for believing this book may be of benefit to others.

FLYE FISHING

What I feel for flye fishing lies in a realm far beyond the power of words to describe.

Affection, love, passion........convenient starting points.

Catching and releasing fish has little to do with it.

Flye fishing is a time and place.

A time and place never to be found; ever to be searched.

The time and place ever closer, ever elusive.

The search is constant, unrelenting.

A time of casts made and fish that took my counterfeit.

It was my choice to release the fish.

It was the place and my companions; the ousel, kingfisher, beaver and deer.

The autumn leaves, riotous in their colours, falling around me.

The wind causing the leaves to dance and flutter; light reflections soothing to the eye.

The vivid sunset drawing the curtain for the day.

The chill in the air halting the search.

The quest continues.

L A Garcia, November 1992

Cover & Rod Building photos by Tony Oswald
Photos by Frank Amato, pages 4 & 47
Photo by Guido Rahr III, page 1
Book and Cover Design by Kathy Johnson
Printed in Hong Kong 10 9 8 7 6 5
ISBN NUMBER: Softbound 1-878175-58-0

TABLE OF CONTENTS

1. Introduction 5

2. Selection of a Blank 6

3. Snake Guides, Stripping Guide(s) Hook Keeper.............7

4. Location of Spline or Spine 9

5. Mounting the Tip Top 10

6. Mounting the Reel Seat 11

   Metal Reel Seat 11

   Components with Cork or Wood Insert 12

   Slip Ring Reel Seat with Wood Insert 13

7. Using the Thompson Rod Wrapping Tool 16

8. Wrapping Without a Tool 18

9. Wrapping the Tip Section 19

   One Thread Wrap 19

   Two Thread Wrap 24

10. The Handle 26

   Using a Finished Handle 26

   Preparing a Handle for Shaping 27

   Shaping the Handle with an Inverted Drill or Lathe.....28

11. Fitting the Winding Check 30

   Rubber 30

   Metallic 30

12. Wrapping the Butt Section 31

13. Fighting the Fuzzies 33

14. Protecting the Wraps 34

15. Finishing the Wraps 35

16. Fly Rod Construction 37

17. Rod Materials List 42

18. Complete Materials List 43

19. Guide Spacings 46

CHAPTER I

INTRODUCTION

My attraction to fly fishing is based on the fact that it requires an understanding of several elements; each of which is related to others; some of which will never be learned completely.

The following comprises a list of elements about which one needs to acquire knowledge to become a proficient flyfisher.

1. Selecting an appropriate fly rod.
2. Selecting an appropriate fly reel.
3. Selecting a matching fly line.
4. Choosing a variety of tapered leaders.
5. Knowing a variety of knots.
6. Knowledge of flies.
7. Skill in making different casts.
8. A rudimentary knowledge of entomology.
9. Knowledge of fly tying materials.
10. Tying equipment and skill in tying flies.

After 18 years of building mostly fly rods and 20 of fly fishing there is much to learn. This, to me, is the most enjoyable aspect of fly fishing. Likewise it is important to recognize that something I thought I knew often requires viewing from a different perspective.

This book will concentrate on only one aspect; rod building. Within the last 18 years of building rods, I have learned some things from which others may benefit and that is the intention of this book. At the time of this writing, I have built over 1200 rods; each of which, I hope, has been built with meticulous care and fastidious attention to detail.

Although I have learned some aspects of bamboo rod building I am most comfortable in discussing graphite since that is the medium through which I have gained most of my experience.

The following is a list of the different manufacturers on whose graphite I have worked.

1. J. Kennedy Fisher
2. Fenwick (Fiberglass & Graphite)
3. Loomis
4. Sage
5. Scott (Restored)
6. R L Winston (Restored)
7. Powell
8. Orvis
9. Clearwater
10. Thomas & Thomas
11. Graphite USA
12. Rodon (Graphite and Boron/Graphite)
13. Diamondback
14. Saint Croix
15. Lamiglas

I have had the privilege of building rods from all the above blanks because I refer to my activity as custom rod building. As such, persons approach me with the desire for a rod and I do what I can to build a rod that suits the need of the individual. Quite often someone will bring me a blank and ask me to complete a rod from that blank. The easiest client for me to please is the one that says "I want you to build me a rod that is X feet long, comes in X sections, casts an X weight line and is made by X company."

For the client who wants a rod but is unsure of the blank several conversations are required. During those conversations we seek answers to questions like:

1. What size rivers do you fish most often?

2. Do you have a preference for rivers of a certain size?

3. What size flies are you required to cast on your favorite waters?

4. Do you prefer to cast flies in a certain size range?

5. Do you prefer a rod with 2, 3 or 4 sections?

6. What kind of "action" do you prefer; slow, medium or fast?

7. What are the size of the fish you catch most often?

8. What are the wind conditions on the waters you fish most often?

9. Do you have a preference for a certain length of rod?

10. Do you have preference for a specific fly line?

11. Are you ready to consider that you may, in fact, need several rods, each of which is intended to solve a specific fishing problem?

While these questions may lead to other questions or discussions, they embody the kind of consultation I employ when talking about a rod for one of my clients.

Rod building is one of several aspects of fly fishing to which one can aspire to learn. It will give you the feeling that you are reaching a higher level of achievement on your way to becoming a Compleat Flye Fisher.

If you are having problems with which you feel I can provide assistance please write to me at:

L A Garcia Rod Company
P O Box 280095
Lakewood, CO 80225-0095

I will respond as quickly as time permits.

CHAPTER 2

SELECTION OF A BLANK

Give yourself adequate time to decide which blank to use. If you need to be judicious with your expenditure you can find blanks that are not expensive. If price is not much of a problem choose a blank made by a well known and reputable manufacturer; their blanks cost more but these costs are justified. Remember they spend a lot of money in research to bring to you the best of their efforts; to do so requires that they spend a lot of money themselves.

Once you decide on a blank for your rod, stay with your decision and do not look back. I have been witness to conversations where one person asked another how come a particular blank was chosen. I have been challenged on my choice of blanks as well. Some will go so far as to insist that so and so makes the "best" blank and that you should build or should have built a rod from that blank. Pick your blank and build your rod. The best blank is the one that feels best to you, period!

The following is a list of manufacturers whose blanks I recommend without hesitation. The list does not include all manufacturers but no attempt has been made to slight anyone. It lists those companies whose blanks I use most often.

Write or call the following companies or find a store in your area that specializes in fly fishing. Try the same store for the other materials needed to complete your rod.

Please refer to Chapters 17 and 18 for materials needed to complete the rod.

J. Kennedy Fisher, Inc
P O Box 3147
Carson City, NV 89702
702 246 5220

Sage Manufacturing
8500 Northeast Day Road
Bainbridge Island, WA 98110
206 842 6608

G. Loomis, Inc.
1359 Downriver Drive
Woodland, WA 98674
206 225 6516

Thomas & Thomas
P O Box 32
Turners Falls, MA 01376
413 863 9727

Powell Rods
P O Box 4000
Chico, CA 95927-4000
1 800 228 0615

Saint Croix Rod Co.
Highway 13 North
Park Falls, WI 54552
1 715 762 3226

It is necessary that you have an idea of the rod length and line weight you want to use. Should there be a question in your mind about either or both then consider a blank that comes in 2 sections, is 9 feet in length and casts a 5 to 6 weight line. With such a rod you will be able to satisfy many of your fishing needs.

I encourage you to build several rods. Try blanks from different manufacturers and draw your own conclusions about the feel of their actions. Rod building is far too enjoyable an activity to just stop at one rod.

If you want ease in transporting your rod then consider one that comes in 3 or 4 sections. When flying outside the country you can take the rod on board thus minimizing the chance of loss or breakage.

The blank used in the photographic sequences was provided by Thomas & Thomas.

The photographs accompanying the text were taken by Tony Oswald.

CHAPTER 3

SNAKE GUIDES, STRIPPING GUIDE(S), HOOK KEEPER

Five kinds of snake guides, of which I am aware, are available for rod crafting. These are:

1. Chrome plated.
2. Unplated stainless steel.
3. Anodized gold.
4. Anodized black.
5. 1 foot guides. (The only ones I know are made by Fuji).Choice depends on taste, preference or practicality.

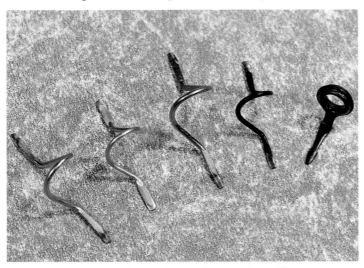

Four snake guides and ceramic guide.

I use the chrome plated variety made by Pacific Bay. Chrome plating provides the hardest surface of which I am currently aware and gives better wear life.

You will find snake guides in a variety of sizes. They start at about 1 and go upward; the larger the number the larger the opening. I have preferred larger guides since 1974 when I built my first rod. The smallest guide I use is a size 2. It is, of course, the snake guide next to the tip top. From there I proceed to a 3, 4, 5 and 6 depending on the rod length and line weight. I have always felt that larger guides create less friction and lead to ease in casting. Although I am not proficient at making long casts, I contend that larger guides allow for longer casts because

of reduced friction. For salt water fly fishing they are, in my opinion, indispensible. I have seen raised eyebrows, and maybe raised hackle, over my choice of guide sizes. Some have challenged my departure from tradition, because, they argue, larger guides are less pleasing to the eye. For my clients I do what they want since my clients are "always right." I always, however, recommend larger guides. I have noticed a trend towards larger guides on some rods and have surmised that others have reached similar conclusions.

Once you have decided on your choice of guides, lay them on the sticky side of masking tape. This helps to keep them in order and prevents their scattering.

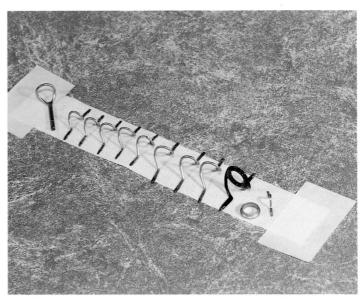

Guides in order.

More often than not each guide and hook keeper requires tapering with a file. A small, hand held, flat mill bastard file will do.

To shape each guide hold it between the thumb and forefinger with the foot up.

Rake the foot across the file, backward and forward, while employing a rocking motion. This will aid in achieving a rounded shape. Do this with moderate speed. If you move your hand too quickly, control is lost and that will lead to undesirable results. It is better, therefore, to start slowly and increase the speed as instinct dictates. Do not be surprised to find a "groove" on your thumb and another on your forefinger. You will also need to touch up the corners of each foot.

Correctly shaped guide with rounded corners and slightly blunt end.

The next photograph illustrates the difference in wrapping results between shaped and unshaped guides.

Properly shaped guide after being wrapped.

Three photos of shaping guide.

This next photo shows the desired result.

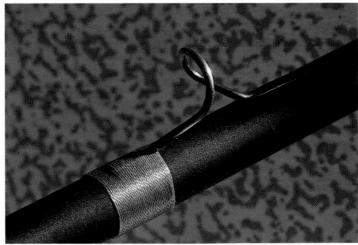

Improperly shaped guide after wrapping.

Perform this task on each snake guide, stripping guide and hook keeper. Return each finished guide to its relative position on the masking tape.

CHAPTER 4

LOCATION OF SPLINE OR SPINE

Each blank has a spline or spine. It is analogous to the backbone in the human body. It results when the graphite is wrapped onto a mandrel. Some portions of the wrap will have slightly more material than others thus resulting in a backbone. Some designs are so well executed that the spline is virtually imperceptible.

What you are trying to find are two "jumps".

Assuming you are using a blank with 2 sections, wrap a piece of masking tape about 1 inch below the tip end of the tip section. Wrap another piece of masking tape about 2 inches below the tip end of the butt section and another one about 5 inches above the butt end of the butt section.

Roll the blank as in the photograph.

Use a pencil or pen to mark the masking tape on the side facing you and where the softer jump occurs. When you wrap the guides you will be wrapping them on the side opposite the mark. This will place the spline on top, both during the backcast and when you are fighting a fish. Some rod builders choose to spline their rods in an opposite manner. They do so to have the backbone predominate during the forward cast.

Proceed to the butt section and perform the same operation. The spline/spine may be very difficult to find on the butt section. If you think you cannot find the spline on the butt section just do the best you can and proceed.

Remember to mark the masking tape closest to the bottom of the butt section. This will be important when mounting the reel seat.

Rolling the blank.

CHAPTER 5

MOUNTING THE TIP TOP

When purchasing materials try several tip tops and find one that is slightly loose but not sloppy. If you order a kit you should get the correct one. After several years of waiting I have found tip tops with large loops. They are now available from Pacific Bay though there may be others.

Scratch the end of the tip with gentle strokes from a very dull knife. The desired result is achieved by scratching the surface just enough to help the epoxy make purchase. Make sure the scratch does not extend below the tip top.

If you can, scratch the inside of the tip top. A fine rattail jewelers file should work. While this step is not essential it helps to ensure that the tip top properly adheres to the blank.

Five minute epoxy is ideal for this job. A drop of resin and one of hardener are more than enough. Stir in one direction for a count of 5; reverse direction for a count of 5; continue alternating the direction in which you stir until you have counted to 40.

Use a needle to put a little epoxy into the opening of the tip top. Use the needle to apply epoxy to the tip. Slide the tip top onto the tip and rotate to spread the epoxy evenly on the inside. Use your finger tip to remove the excess. Align the mark on the masking tape with the tip top as in the accompanying photograph.

Stand the tip vertically and allow to sit 24 hours.

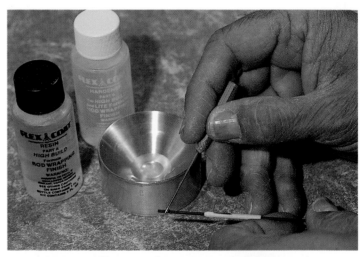

Using needle to apply epoxy to tip of tip section.

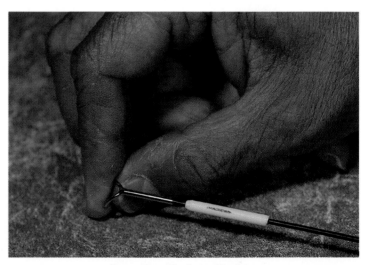

Inserting tip into tip top.

After an overnight set pull and twist on the tip top to ensure proper adhesion. As long as your epoxy mixture is correct you should not have to worry about the tip coming off.

Remove the masking tape with the mark on it and discard. The tip top will become your point of reference when wrapping the snake guides.

Using needle to apply epoxy to inside of tip top.

CHAPTER 6

MOUNTING THE REEL SEAT

Four examples will be provided in this chapter; they are from left to right:

1. All metal reel seat with brown anodizing.
2. Down locking with polished aluminum fittings and wood insert.
3. Down locking with brown aluminum fittings and wood insert.
4. Up locking with polished aluminum fittings and wood insert.
5. Up locking with cork insert, fighting butt extension and polished aluminum fittings.

Five Reel Seats.

If I do not have a specific example for a reel seat you may have in mind, it is because I do not have every reel seat available. My examples, however, should help solve some situations not otherwise noted.

Metal Reel Seat

For this type of reel seat masking tape is needed. Most any width will do but 3/4 inch seems to work best.

Wrap just enough to ensure the reel seat slides smoothly into place over the masking tape.

The first wrap is made about 1/4 inch from the bottom of the butt section.

The second wrap is made about 1/4 inch down from what will be the top of the reel seat.

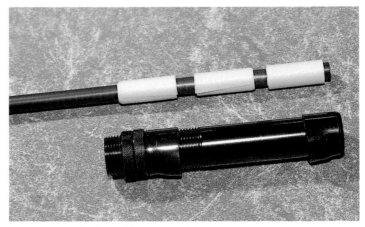

Reel seat lying next to wraps to show relationship of wraps.

Use a rattail file to scratch the inside of the metal reel seat. This helps to ensure adhesion.

Rattail file scratching inside of reel seat.

Make a wrap of masking tape on the outside of the reel seat. Make a mark down the centerline on the side opposite where the reel is to be mounted. This mark will be used as an alignment with the spline/spine of the blank made in Chapter 4.

Mix about a teaspoon each of resin and hardener of 5 minute epoxy. Apply a generous amount, a little at a time, to the inside of the reel seat. Slide the blank into the reel seat up to the first wrap of masking tape. Apply a ring of epoxy all around the tape; rotate the blank and push inward. The epoxy will tend to push outward. As this happens hold the blank vertically so the epoxy flows back into the inside of the reel seat. Apply some epoxy to the forward wrap of masking tape. Once again the epoxy will tend to push ahead and out of the top end of the reel seat. This makes vertical orientation of the blank all the more important. This will help the epoxy move back into the opening of the reel seat and into the 1/4 inch gap you left below the top of the reel seat.

Epoxy into metal reel seat.

Align the mark made on top of the reel seat with the mark made on the masking tape back in Chapter 4 during location of the spline/spine. This ensures alignment of the reel seat with the spline/spine of the blank.

It is fastidious attention to details such as this that distinguishes a rod builder's craft.

Let the section stand vertically overnight.

Example of alignment with vertical orientation.

Components With Cork Or Wood Insert

This installation is relatively easy.

These instructions, with little changes, should work whether you are using an uplocking or downlocking reel seat.

You will either need to wrap enough masking tape on the blank to equal the borehole of the insert or ream out the insert with a rattail file.

Wrapping Masking Tape To Equal The Borehole Of The Insert

These instructions are virtually the same as those used for installation of the all metal reel seat.

Make sure your wrap is about 1/4th of an inch above the butt end of the blank and the other is about 1/4th of an inch down from the top of the cork or wood insert.

Mix about a teaspoon each of resin and hardener of 5 minute epoxy. Apply a generous amount, a little at a time, to the inside of the reel seat. Slide the blank into the reel seat up to the first wrap of masking tape. Apply a ring of epoxy all around the tape; rotate the blank and push inward. The epoxy will tend to push outward. As this happens hold the blank vertically so the epoxy flows back into the inside of the reel seat. Apply some epoxy to the forward wrap of masking tape. Once again the epoxy will tend to push ahead and out of the top end of the reel seat. This makes vertical orientation of the blank all the more important. This will help the epoxy move back into the opening of the reel seat and into the 1/4 inch gap you left below the top of the reel seat.

Let the section stand vertically overnight.

Reaming Out The Borehole Of The Cork Or Wood Insert

Start by reaming out the borehole of the cork or wood insert. Ream out the borehole until the insert slides all the way to the bottom of the butt section. There should be a little "play." This will allow for a smooth spreading of the epoxy between the insert and the wall of the shaft.

Wrap masking tape around the insert and mark its centerline on the side opposite where the reel is to be placed. Use this mark to align the reel seat with the spline/spine of the blank.

Next, mix 5 minute epoxy and set the upper part of the reel seat *first.*

Allow the epoxy to set.

Photo of front part of reel seat in place.

Next, mix 5 minute epoxy and apply it to the blank *about* 4 inches from the bottom of the blank. Bring down the first part of the reel seat. Rotate the reel seat to allow even spreading of the epoxy.

Photo of reel seat at bottom of blank.

Immediately install the bottom piece of the reel seat. Put about a 1/4 inch ring of epoxy at the bottom of the bottom piece and push the insert into place. Be sure to align the bottom piece with the front piece and the spline/spine of the blank. Put your reel in place momentarily to ensure it fits properly. Remove the reel.

Photo of complete reel seat in place.

Allow the epoxy to set.

If you use a cork insert, *and intend to shape your own handle,* protect it by wrapping one turn of paper around the outside of the insert, then wrap masking tape over the paper to hold the paper in place. This will prevent adhesives in the masking tape from damaging the cork.

Paper wrap around cork insert.

Slip Ring Reel Seat With Wood Insert

Components for slip ring reel seat.

These instructions are similar to the ones needed to install a components reel seat with cork or wood insert.

They are provided because of the difference in the physical features of the slip ring reel seat.

Because of the unique design of the Struble slip ring reel seat, exercise care in orienting the components properly.

Mix about a teaspoon each of resin and hardener of 5 minute epoxy. Put about a 1/8 inch ring at the very bottom of the bottom piece.

Putting epoxy at bottom of bottom piece of slip ring reel seat.

Putting epoxy into reel seat.

Bring the wood insert down into the bottom piece. This will keep the epoxy from leaking out. Put the reel in place *momentarily* to ensure proper placement. Remove the reel.

Put the seat aside vertically and allow the epoxy to set.

After the epoxy is set put the slip ring in place. Make sure the slip ring is oriented properly.

Slip ring in place correctly.

Mix about a drop each of resin and hardener of 5 minute epoxy. Use a needle to apply a small amount to the underside of the top piece of the reel seat. Put the top piece of the reel seat in place.

Allow the epoxy to set.

Because of the design of the reel seat, mounting of the reel is not necessary. You may, however, want to mount the reel to give you an idea of how it will look.

Mix about a teaspoon each of resin and hardener of 5 minute epoxy. Apply a generous amount, a little at a time, to the inside of the reel seat. Slide the blank into the reel seat. Rotate the blank and push inward. The epoxy will tend to push outward. As this happens hold the blank vertically so the epoxy flows back into the

Vertical Insertion.

Set the seat aside and allow the epoxy to set.

Because this reel seat is grooved you must make a modification to it if you use this reel seat and decide to shape your own handle.

Cut 5 to 6 pieces of 1/2 inch wide masking tape to about 2 inches in length. Lay each piece of masking tape into the groove, one over the other, until enough have been laid to make a smooth transition between the wood and the groove. This will help ensure the handle is as round as possible.

Abel reel in place.

Tape in groove.

Overwrap of masking over tape in groove.

CHAPTER 7

USING THE THOMPSON ROD WRAPPING TOOL

If you decide to wrap with 2 colors of thread, you will need 2 tools. The tool is designed to hold 1 spool.

Find a table or bench onto which you can clamp the tool or tools.

Open the spool holder using the thumb of your left hand to facilitate the process.

Pull thread from the spool while pressing down gently with the thumb of your left hand as in the photograph.

Opening the spool holder.

Insert the spool while continuing to use the thumb of your left hand. You may need to ream out the bore-hole of the spool.

Inserting the spool.

Pulling thread from the spool holder.

Adjusting tension of the tool.

Adjust the tension against the spool with the left hand as in the photograph. Because of the tool's design it is probably best to adjust the tool by this means even though you may be right handed. Adjust the tension so that the thread is taunt. You will, of course, need to experiment till you find an adjustment that suits you. Further adjustments may be made anytime.

CHAPTER 8

WRAPPING WITHOUT A TOOL

A phone book or dictionary will get the job done. For tension adjustment, stack more books on top.

Drop the spool or spools into small glass containers like those in which you find baby food or jelly.

Place the thread(s) close to the binding; the closer to the binding the better. This will help keep tension as you wrap. You should avoid a loose wrap because the guides may "drift" during use.

You are ready to wrap.

Setup for wrapping without a tool.

WRAPPING THE TIP SECTION

An empty cardboard box with notches cut on each side will do the job. The notches will cradle the blank while you wrap. Simple and it works.

The following photograph shows a simple wrapping rig I made and used for years. You can build something like this with spare pieces of lumber you are likely to have laying around the house.

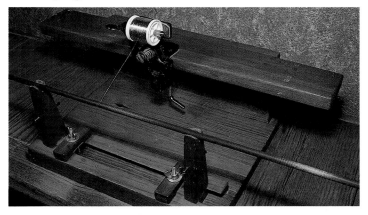

First wrapping rig.

The following photograph shows the wrapping tool I use today. It is still simple but more functional because of the size and the drawers that allow storage of frequently needed materials.

Current wrapping rig.

Practice on a spare piece of graphite before wrapping the rod.

One Thread Wrap

The tip top is now in place and secured.

Cut thin strips of masking tape and use them to mark the blank where the guides are to be placed.

Wrap the strips on the blank where the guides are to be located.

Use the guide spacings recommended by the manufacturer of the blank you are using.

If you cannot find guide spacings use those provided in Chapter 19.

Use the edge of the masking tape closest to the tip to indicate the mark. This will be the "leading edge".

Use the leading edge of the masking tape to mark the remaining guide placements.

When placing the snake guide for wrapping, make sure the apex of the guide crosses the leading edge of the masking tape and is as closely aligned with the tip top as possible.

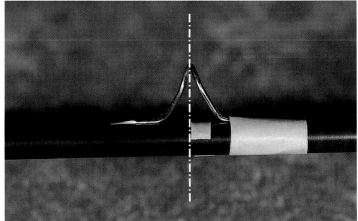

Apex of guide aligned with leading edge of masking tape and with tip top.
(Stripe indicates vertical alignment.)

Secure one foot with masking tape. The opposite foot is wrapped. The wrap starts on the blank and proceeds onto the foot of the guide.

Start the wrap about 2/16 to 3/16 of an inch from the end of the foot. Cut a piece of card stock to the exact measurement you want. Lay the card stock against the foot of the guide. The opposite edge marks where the wrap is to begin. With the card stock you will have a consistent measurement for *all* wraps.

Card stock against guide.

Bring the free end of thread over the top of the blank. The thread will hang down in front of you. Allow about 8 inches to hang down. With one hand reach over the top and behind the blank, grasp the thread and bring it over the top of the blank and back toward you. This completes the first turn of thread around the blank.

Full view of first turn of thread.

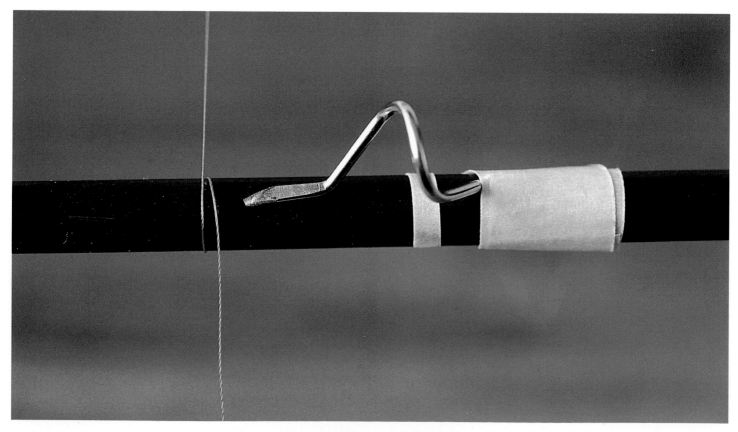

Closeup of first turn of thread.

Now make sure the thread coming off the spool crosses over the top of the thread you are holding in your hand. Canting the blank makes the crossover easy.

As you proceed into the second turn of thread you will find it necessary to hold your thumb against the wrap, otherwise the thread will unravel. Pulling the free end of the thread is also required to tighten the wrap against the blank. Continue holding the thumb against the wrap and pulling the free end of the thread. This ensures a tight wrap against the blank. Make 5 to 8 turns of thread in this manner.

By now you are getting close to the foot of the guide. Grab the free end of the thread and hold it with one hand. With the free hand pick up the scissors and cut the free end of the thread. Use your fingernail to push the wraps as close to each other as possible. Keep subsequent turns of thread tightly against each other.

Full view of canting.

Full view of cutting the thread.

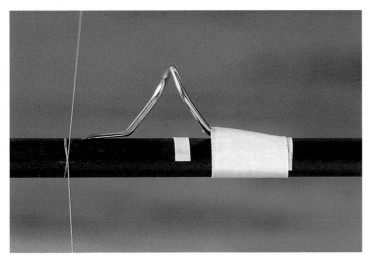

Closeup of canting.

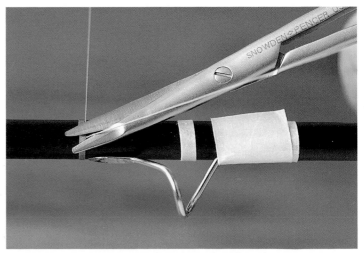

Closeup of cutting the thread.

Continue wrapping until you have made about 5 to 8 turns onto the foot of the guide. This will secure the guide to the blank. Now lay in your whip finishing tool on the side *opposite* the guide and make 2 wraps to keep it in place. The whip finisher will stay in place until the wrap is finished.

Continue wrapping until the thread reaches the curve of the guide. Now press your thumb against the blank at the point where the thread meets the whip finisher.

Pull thread from the spool and cut it off at about 8 inches. Pass the free end of the thread through the loop of the whip finisher. Do not release the thumb pressure.

Full view of laying in whip finisher.

Full view of passing thread through loop.

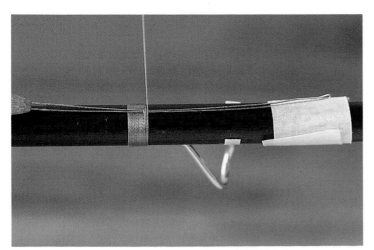

Closeup of laying in whip finisher.

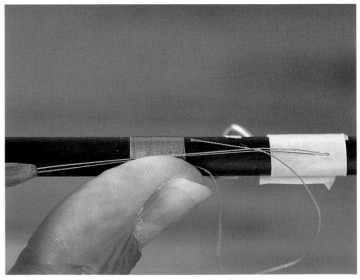

Closeup of passing thread through loop.

Now wrap the free end of thread around the forefinger of your free hand and put steady pressure against the wrap.

Pull the whip finisher until it is about 7 turns of thread *under* the wrap.

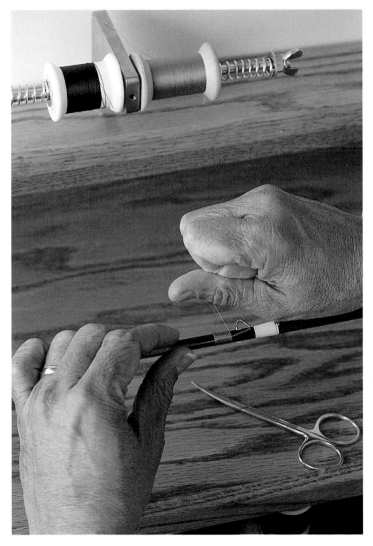

Full view of pulling thread.

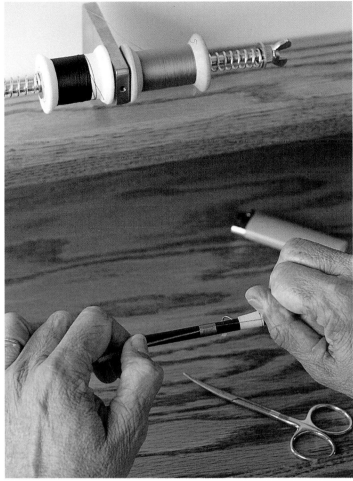

Full view of whip finisher under wrap.

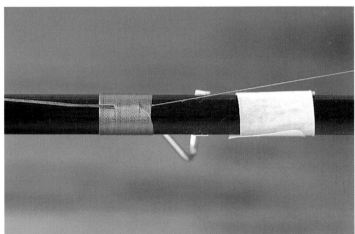

Closeup of whip finisher under wrap.

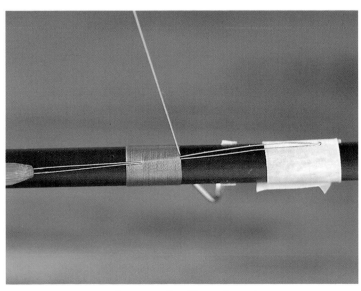

Closeup of pulling thread.

Now pull the whip finisher in one direction and the thread that is wrapped around your forefinger in the opposite direction with *equal* pressure. Continue pulling in opposite directions until the thread ruptures underneath the wrap. Both the whip finisher and loose end of thread will emerge from underneath the wrap.

This method minimizes "fuzzies." See Chapter 13.

Check the alignment of the guide with the tip top. If necessary force the guide into alignment. If this process seems very difficult it is best to un-wrap and re-wrap the guide.

Proceed wrapping the remaining guides on the tip section in the same manner.

Forcing guide into position.

Check alignment of subsequent guides with the adjoining one.

Careful attention to detail will ensure correct alignment of all guides.

Two other wraps are recommended: one adjacent to the tip top and one at the bottom of the tip section. They are pleasing to the eye and practical because they reinforce high stress points.

For rods with a ferruling system like those found on Sage, Loomis, Powell and Saint Croix a wrap of about 2

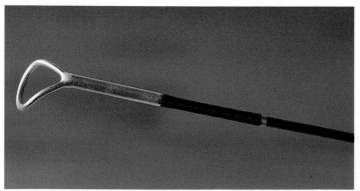

Tip top wrap.

End of tip section wrap.

inches is suggested at the the bottom of the *tip* section. This provides relief at a high stress point.

Two Thread Wrap

Practice on a spare piece of graphite before proceeding to wrap the rod if you decide to use the two thread wrap.

Remember, you will need 2 spools of thread for this wrap. If you are using a Thompson Rod Wrapping tool, you will need 2 of them. Put the contrast color on the **right** and the base color on the **left**. This implies wrapping from left to right for a person who is right handed.

Start with the contrast color.

Follow the same steps as in the 1 thread wrap. Count the number of turns of thread around the blank. With the 2 color thread wrap, or continuous wrap as I call it, you can make as few as 1 turn of thread or as many as you like. Four to six turns seem to work best. Experiment to determine the number of turns you like best.

After you have made the number of turns of thread you want to use, reach for the other thread and bring it forward to join the first thread.

Lay the thread over the one that is already wrapped and hold it in place with pressure from your thumb.

Notice the "V" formed between the 2 threads.

Thread join and "V" formation.

You may need to create slack for this next step. As long as you keep pressure with your thumb against the wrap, the wrap will stay in place. Push your free hand into the "V" and grasp the *new* thread. Pull your hand out of the "V" bringing the thread with it. Keep the thumb pressed against the junction of the two threads. Your first turn of the new thread is now in place.

Cut off the contrasting thread about 8 inches from the junction. Keep the thumb placed against the junction of the 2 threads. Continue wrapping the new thread until you have made about 5 to 7 turns of the new thread. The new thread is now holding down the first thread. That is why I call it the continuous wrap. Now you have 3 strands of thread hanging. Two of them are of the first thread and one of the new thread. Carefully unravel the free ends and pull on them with an upward motion.

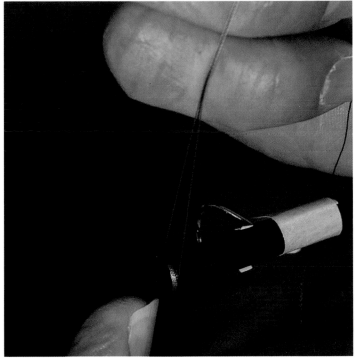

Pulling 3 threads with an upward motion.

This tightens the wrap and pushes each turn of thread against the other.

Now cut the 3 loose strands of thread.

Make about 6 more turns of thread and lay in the whip finisher.

Complete the wrap as previously instructed.
Proceed to the other wraps using the same technique.

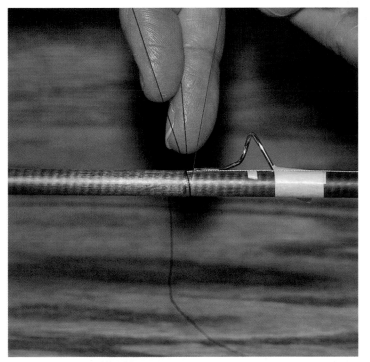

Hand inside "V" formation.

Three threads after they have been cut off.

CHAPTER 10

THE HANDLE

Using a finished handle represents a considerable savings in time and trouble. It should be quite easy to find finished handles where you find other rod building components.

Finished handles are available from Glenn Struble Manufacturing. You will find address and phone information in Chapter 18, Item 3.

The handles you see in the accompanying photograph were loaned from Struble Manufacturing.

Finished handles. 10-1

From left to right they are:

A. Wells

This handle shape may be used for traditional downlocking reel seats as well as uplocking reel seats. For uplocking reel seats it is just about an absolute must to prevent exposure of the hood that holds the front foot of the reel. The front hood is almost always recessed into the bottom-most cork ring.

B. Half Wells

This handle shape is used mostly with downlocking reel seats. For uplocking reel seats it does not work as well because there is a risk of removing so much cork at the bottom that the front hood is exposed. The front hood accepts the front foot of the reel and is recessed into the bottom-most cork ring.

C. Reverse half Wells

This handle shape may be used for traditional downlocking reel seats as well as uplocking reel seats. For uplocking reel seats it is just about an absolute must to prevent exposure of the hood that holds the front foot of the reel. The front hood is almost always recessed into the bottom-most cork ring.

D. Cigar

This is probably the most used handle shape. It is also, in my opinion, the most practical and, consequently, the one I use most often. With a sufficient number of cork rings (13, 14, 15, or more) it allows the hand to move fore and aft during a long day of casting. As the hand and forearm tire we move the hand up and down the handle without even knowing we are doing it. Subconsciously we move the hand to relieve fatigue. With the cigar shape we have a lot of freedom about where we hold the handle; less so with other handle shapes. Handles with curves **tend** to make us keep our hands in certain positions.

E. Reverse half Wells with Fine Point.

This handle shape may be used for traditional downlocking reel seats as well as uplocking reel seats. For uplocking reel seats it is just about an absolute must to prevent exposure of the hood that holds the front foot of the reel. The front hood is almost always recessed into the bottom-most cork ring. This handle shape is very good for fly rods in the 2, 3 and 4 weight category. It allows the person to put their finger tip at the junction of the handle with the blank, increasing sensitivity to delicate strikes.

If you find a handle whose borehole allows the handle to slide freely to within 12 inches from where it will rest, you are really fortunate. You do not want it to slide freely to where it rests. This creates too much of a chance for less than a snug fit. If there is not enough adhesion at all points, top to bottom, there is a chance the handle will "squeak" during casting. You may conclude that the graphite is cracked and while that may be true it is not likely. It is more likely that cork is rubbing against the blank and it is non uniform contact with the blank that produces the "squeak".

Ream out the borehole with a rattail file so that the handle slides freely to a point about 8 inches from where it will rest. What you are trying to achieve is to remove enough cork so that the epoxy is spread evenly from top to bottom between the handle and the blank. Make a crayola mark, on the blank, at the top of the handle. Move the handle back up the blank.

Mix about a tablespoon each of resin and hardener of 5 minute epoxy. Put a ring of epoxy about 1/8th of an inch in width on the blank below the crayola mark.

Three finished handles in place.

Bring the handle down to where you put epoxy. As you push toward the reel seat twist the handle to ensure the epoxy is spread uniformly. Keep putting epoxy and pushing and twisting the handle till it comes to rest on top of the reel seat. As long as you leave a gap at the top of the reel seat the epoxy will enter the gap and make good adhesion. At best you can hope that the epoxy is as evenly spread as possible. Later, if there are squeaks during casting, you will know what happened. You may or may not need to erase the crayola mark.

Allow sufficient time for the epoxy to set.

Preparing A Handle For Shaping

If you are inexperienced or uncomfortable with this idea please consider using a finished handle. Refer back to the first part of this chapter. If you have decided to shape your own handle I applaud you for your decision.

You have chosen a more difficult route. Shaping a handle directly on the blank is risky! If you make a serious error you will need to remove the cork, clean the surface as best you can and install new rings. Even though it is a more difficult route I feel it is closer to artistry in rod building.

While length and shape are a matter of personal taste, please consider a handle with a minimum of 13 rings for rods 6 to 8 feet in length and 14 rings for rods 8 1/2 to 9 1/2 feet in length. You may even want to use longer handles. I contend that longer handles are more practical, irrespective of the size of a persons hand. My conclusion is based on the following observations. During a day of casting I find myself moving my hand up and down on the handle. I believe this happens because as the day progresses the wrist and forearm become fatigued. To alleviate fatigue the hand creeps up and down on the handle. I am convinced I do this unconsciously. I have observed this behavior in others and suspect they do it for the same reason. Because of these observations I have concluded that the cigar shaped handle allows for greater freedom in moving the hand fore and aft.

If you decide to use an uplocking handle you will *just about* have to consider a full Wells or reversed half Wells shape, because you need to stay away from the hood where the front foot of the reel is attached. You can still use a cigar shaped handle but you must be careful about removing too much cork and exposing the hood. Also, the bottom ring will need to have some cork removed to accept the hood of the reel seat where the front foot of the reel is placed. Struble uplocking reel seats come with the cork ring already reamed out to accept the hood.

Inspect each ring carefully. Choose the 2 rings that appear to have the highest density and smoothness of surface. One will rest at the top of the reel seat and the other at the top of the handle.

Begin by reaming out the ring that will sit on top of the reel seat. Ream the ring so that it slides freely to a point about 12 inches from where it will rest. This will cause you to push the ring into place. A tight fit is what you want—a fit tight enough so that there is complete contact between the cork and blank. Push the ring to where it will rest on top of the reel seat. If you use a Struble uplocking reel seat remember that the first cork ring is part of the reel seat.

Ream out the remaining rings, each less than the one before it to ensure a tight fit. The last one is reserved to sit at the top of the handle.

Now slide each ring back up the blank but do not take them off.

Mix about a soupspoon each of resin and hardener epoxy. I like to stir in one direction to a slow count of 10; reverse direction for a count of 10 and repeat the process till I have counted to 40. This ensures proper mixture. I use Rod Builders Epoxy Glue from Flex Coat for this operation. See Chapter 18, Item 4 for address and phone information.

Put about an 1/8 inch ring of epoxy around the blank about 1/8 of an inch *above* the reel seat. Bring the first ring down and rotate it to ensure uniform spreading of the epoxy around the blank. Any epoxy pushing ahead will move into the gap you left at the top of the reel seat.

Thereafter, spread a *film* of epoxy on the surface of the ring, making sure that some of the epoxy makes contact with the blank. This ensures complete contact and adhesion. Now bring the next ring down to meet the one that is in place. Rotate the newly positioned ring for uniform spreading of the epoxy. Push each ring hard against the other to minimize gaps between rings.

Continue until all rings are in place.

Set the handle aside for 24 hours.

Shaping The Handle With An Inverted Drill Or Lathe

Use 3/4 inch masking tape. Cut a section about 12 inches long. Wrap it about 1/8 of an inch below the *tip* end of the butt section.

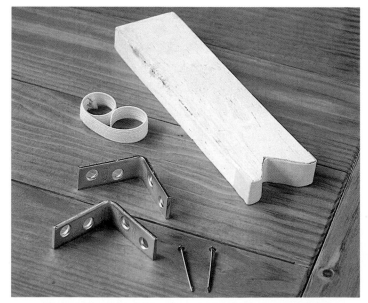

Items 28, 29 and 39, Chapter 18, before assembly.

Support the butt end.

If you do not have access to a lathe use items 28, 29 and 39 as described in Chapter 18. Be careful to make sure the support is as level as possible. Correct leveling assures the handle is round when the handle is complete. I built many rods using this setup before graduating to an expensive lathe.

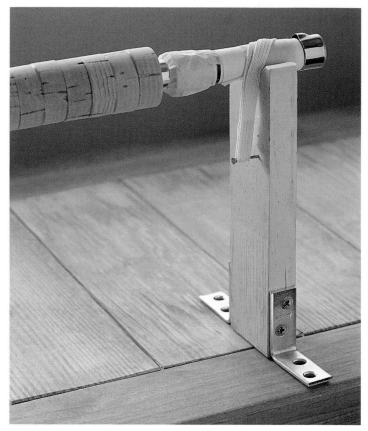

After assembly.

If you have access to a lathe, it should have a support for the butt end.

Remember to protect the insert of the reel seat with masking tape during the shaping of the handle.

Insert the tip end into the drill or lathe chuck. Tighten on the masking tape with enough pressure to keep the tip in place during the turning operation. Be careful not to over-tighten and risk collapsing the blank.

Tightening tip end of butt section into chuck.

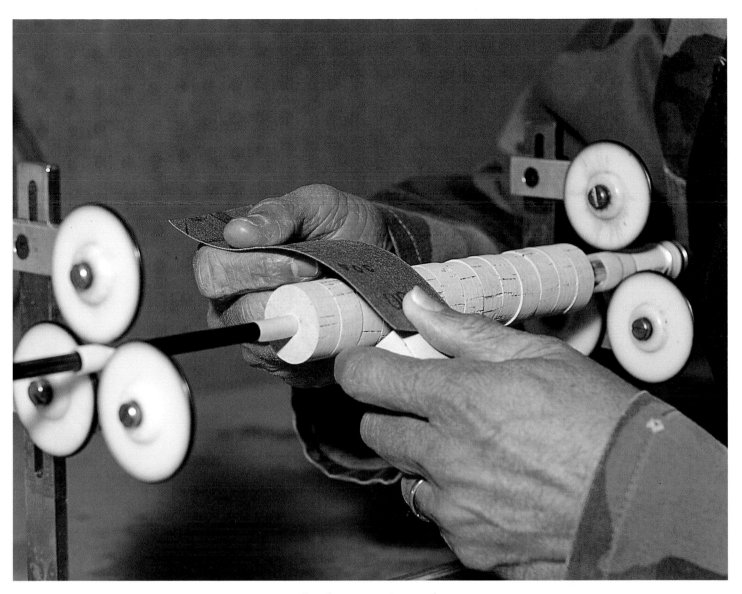

Sandpaper against cork.

If you do not have a shop vac to capture the cork dust, please use a mask of some sort.

You are ready to turn on the drill or lathe.

Use one hand to hold the blank immediately above the handle. The other hand is free to do the shaping.

With a lathe you should be able to provide support to the blank midpoint between the tip and butt end. This is necessary to prevent a midpoint wobble. Wrap this point as well. Both hands should be free.

Start shaping with the 60 grit paper; take your time!

Continue with the 60 grit until you get *close* to the shape you want, then stop.

Change to the 100 grit and continue shaping to get *very close* to the desired shape, then stop.

Now use the Birch/Fir putty to fill holes in the cork.

Change to the 220 grit paper. What you want now is *smoothing* and *finishing.* Stop and check your work often. It's likely you will need more putty as you proceed through this phase.

Best of luck with this most difficult part.

If you feel you are making or have made a serious error in shaping the handle then *stop.* You will, very likely, have to remove the cork, clean the blank as best you can and start a new handle.

CHAPTER 11

FITTING THE WINDING CHECK

ow that the reel seat and handle are in place you are ready to install the winding check.

Two rubber winding checks.

Rubber Winding Check

If you decide on rubber as in the preceeding photo, look for one that slides to within a few inches (4 to 10) from the top of the handle. Let it slide to that point then simply push it down to where it rests on top of the handle; it is no more complex than that.

Rubber winding check in place.

Metallic Winding Check

If you decide on a metal winding check, search carefully for one that slides to within 1/2 to 2 inches from the top of the handle; the closer the better. Once in a while you will find one that fits just the way you want.

I use winding checks from Struble Manufacturing.

See Chapter 18, Item 3 for address and phone information.

For the metal winding check you will need a reaming tool such as:

1. Reamer
2. Moto Tool.

Remove very little metal and test the fit. Continue carefully until the winding check fits snugly on top of the handle *without* having to push the winding check into position.

Adhesive is *not* recommended. Adhesive may leak out from underneath the winding check and create cleaning problems with which you should not have to deal. When you wrap the hook keeper the wrap will hold the winding check in place and it *will not* move.

Metallic winding check in place.

Remember also that you will be applying a finish to the wrap and it will further secure the winding check to the top of the handle.

Set the winding check aside. You will not wrap the winding check until you get to Chapter 12.

WRAPPING THE BUTT SECTION

Position the winding check at the top of the handle. I suggest you wrap the hook keeper first. The usual place is adjacent to the winding check. Wrap the hook keeper where you feel it best serves your needs; on top, left side, right side or bottom. The bottom position seems to best place the winding check out of the way.

Hook keepers

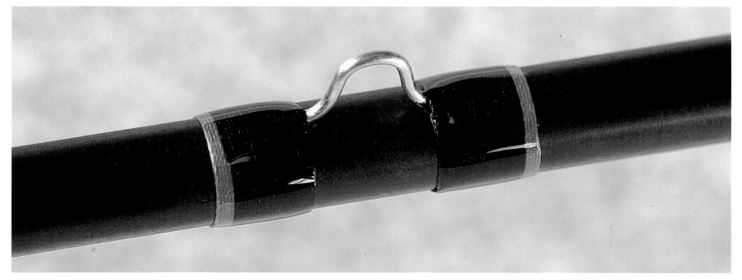

Standard

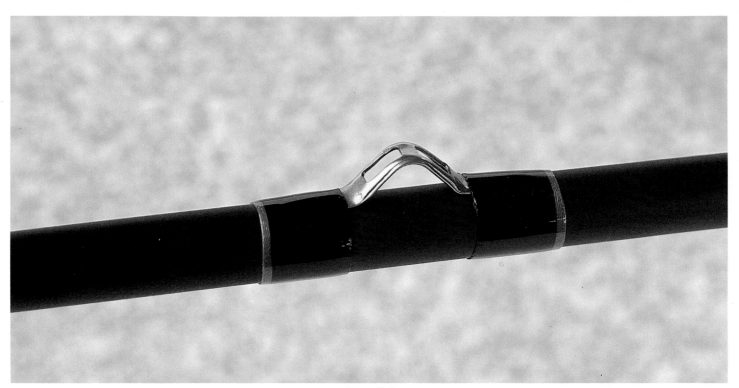

Fenwick

Hook and ring.

Next wrap the stripping guide closest to the reel. Mount an empty reel on the reel seat and align the stripping guide with the reel. To help the alignment I turn the rod so that the reel is on top and I can look through the middle of an empty reel to the center of the stripping guide.

If you want to get **adventurous** rotate the stripping guide closest to the reel about 20 degrees to the right or left of alignment with the reel. Which direction you rotate depends on whether you are a right or left handed caster. For a right handed caster rotate to the left. For a left handed caster rotate to the right. This rotates the first stripping guide closer to the line hand, reducing both friction and static electricity during casting. If you use this technique, alignment of the first stripping guide with the spline/spine of the rod is not necessary.

Do the very best you can to ensure proper alignment. This will help minimize forcing the guide into alignment after the wrap is completed.

Remove the reel before wrapping.

Place the reel back on after both sides of the wrap are complete. Check the alignment. If necessary force the guide to align with the reel. Do this with care!

For rods 6 to 8 feet in length there may be 1 or 2 more guide(s) to wrap, depending on the guide spacings you are using. If 3 guides are suggested for the butt section I use 2 stripping guides and one snake guide. For salt water rods I recommend 3 stripping guides. If only 2 guides are suggested for the butt section than the one closest to the reel will be a stripping guide and the one closest to the tip will be a snake guide. I use the largest guides possible. As mentioned elsewhere I am convinced large guides reduce friction, static electricity and lead to longer casts.

Complete wrapping the butt section, aligning subsequent guides relative to the centerline of the blank using an empty reel to aid in alignment. If you did get **adventurous,** as suggested in a preceeding paragraph, the second and/or third guide(s) should be aligned with the centerline of the rod.

If necessary please refer to Chapter 9 for wrapping instructions.

If you are building a rod that has a ferrule such as that found on Fisher blanks or the Thomas & Thomas blank used in the preparation of this book, I encourage you to make a wrap on either side of the internal ferrule (also called a spigot ferrule). Mark a section of about 1 inch on either side of the ferrule and wrap. This will give the ferrule a symmetrical look and is practical since both sides of the ferrule are high stress points.

For rods that come in 3 or 4 sections, reinforcing wraps are suggested at each joint.

CHAPTER 13

FIGHTING THE FUZZIES

The rod is just about ready. The tip top is in place, the reel seat is in place, the handle is ready, the wrapping is complete and now we come to the finishing stages.

For "fighting the fuzzies" you will need a cigarette lighter, alcohol lamp and if all else fails, a match will do. The butane type cigarette lighter seems to be the best inexpensive alternative.

"Fuzzies" are minute strands of thread sometimes left protruding between the wraps. So minute are they, at times, that you cannot see them until you have completely finished the wrap. If you have not detected the fuzzies until then, your reaction will be less than civil.

Hold the flame to the *side* of the wrap that is most comfortable to you!

If you hold the heat source *above* the wrap you will not get enough heat.

If you hold the heat source *under* the wrap the threads may rupture and unravel!

If you do not find and remove the fuzzies the example in the photo *will* result.

I use a 10X magnifier to inspect each and every wrap to help me avoid the horror.

The *only* logical option is to remove the wrap and do it all over again!

If this happens use a thin bladed knife with a *dull* blade. Lay the blade flat against the blank, move the dull edge up to the wrap then push against the wrap and use an upward motion (away from the blank). Eventually the thread will lift up so you can grasp it with tweezers or your fingers. Now you can unwind the wrap and rub the surface with your fingernail to remove all debris; rub the blank with a tissue soaked in alcohol or acetone until it is as smooth as it can possibly be. At this point you are ready to re-wrap.

With careful attention to detail during the wrapping process you will *not have to fight the fuzzies*

Fuzzies showing through finished wrap.

CHAPTER 14

PROTECTING THE WRAPS

I f you want to be totally comfortable with your decision about protecting the wraps, find a spare piece of graphite, make several small wraps, and experiment.

Whether you use varnish followed by epoxy, epoxy over epoxy or thread sealer followed by epoxy, your choice should be a personal one. Please review the information in this chapter before deciding which method you prefer.

Some rod builders choose not to use sealer; I do. I use Color Preserver and Thread Sealer from Roger Seiders at Flex Coat and have been using it for years. I use it straight from the container and apply it with brushes also available from Flex Coat. Stir or swirl; do not shake! Shaking puts a lot of bubbles in the sealer and you will have to fight the bubbles when you apply the sealer to the wraps.

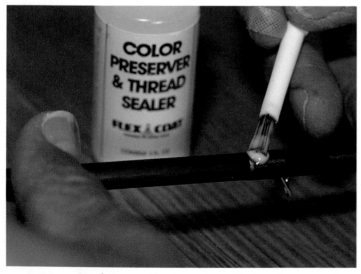

Applying sealer to wrap with brush.

Were I to use a 1 colour thread wrap I would probably not use sealer. Since I insist on doing a 2 colour thread wrap I feel a need for thread sealer.

Here are the consequences. If you *do not* use thread sealer and apply either varnish or epoxy directly to the thread, the varnish or epoxy will soak into the thread

and change its colour characteristics. After drying you can lay the original spool of thread next to the wrap and you will notice a distinct difference in the coloration of both. More often than not the varnish or epoxy will darken the thread. This becomes quite apparent with lighter colored threads. In the darker colored threads you may not notice any difference.

In the next photograph the wraps are identical, that is a black wrap with gold trim. The wrap on the left was done with 1 coat of varnish, the one in the middle with 1 coat of Flex Coat epoxy and the one on the right with 3 coats of sealer. Decide on the one you like best and go with it. I want a colour differentiation between the 2 threads and get the results I want by using thread sealer.

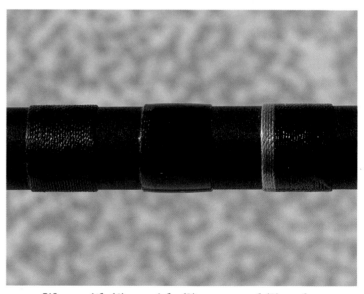

Wrap with (1) varnish, (2) epoxy and (3) sealer.

It is difficult to tell how many coats you will need. If you decide on varnish consider applying 2 protecting coats of varnish. If you decide on epoxy consider applying 1 protecting coat of epoxy. If you decide on Flex Coat thread sealer consider applying 2 to 3 coats. The sealer will have a glossy appearance.

There are also NCP (No Color Preserver) threads. While I have tried them I have not experienced the results I demand.

CHAPTER 15

FINISHING THE WRAPS

ake Sure you have about two hours of free time before you start this phase of completion!

Note: Find yourself an empty cardboard box wide enough to hold each section of the rod. Cut notches on either side of the box to cradle each section. It is all you need.

Whether or not you use varnish only, epoxy only or thread sealer for the initial coat of finish, this step will be the same; that is the final coat should be epoxy. It produces a glossy coat whose surface is hard and lasting.

If you have laid down a good base of varnish, epoxy or sealer you *should* only need 1 coat of epoxy. If you are using the newer thin epoxies, I cannot predict what results you will experience.

If you are experimenting do so on a spare piece of graphite, *not on the rod you are nearing completion.*

I use High Build Polymer Rod Wrapping Finish from Flex Coat.

To achieve best results I use 3 cc syringes. The Flex Coat formula comes with and without syringes. I recommend the one that includes the syringes. One half cc of each is all you need if you follow my suggestion about not finishing more than 6 wraps at a time.

I mix 1/2 cc from each syringe in a mixing bowl available from Jack Perry. See Chapter 18, Item 30 for address and phone information.

I then take a knitting needle and stir *slowly* for 2 minutes. I first stir in one direction for a count of 10; reverse direction for a count of 10 and repeat this process until I have counted to 120. This is about a 2 minute stir. Stir *slowly* to minimize putting bubbles into the mixture. Bubbles make finishing very difficult. The difficulty may be minimized by using a cigarette lighter to burst the bubbles after the epoxy is on the wrap.

As soon as you have completed the stirring process you can start applying epoxy to the wraps.

I apply the epoxy *only* to the thread; never to the blank. I prefer this because I find it most pleasing to the eye. I also find it easier to re-wrap a rod whose finish only covers the thread.

You may want to allow the epoxy to overlap onto the blank as well; that is, the area immediately adjacent to the wrap. The accompanying photograph should help you decide on a personal preference.

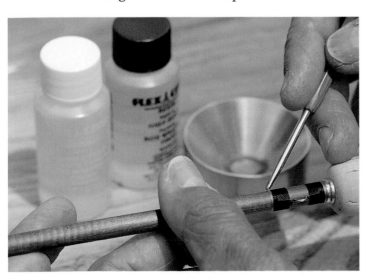

Applying epoxy to wraps.

Finish on wraps only versus finish on the blank as well.

Laser engraved reel seat.

I recommend you apply epoxy to no more than 6 guides or 12 wraps at a time. You may want to try more. While it may take more time to complete the rod it produces excellent results. The problem is that the epoxy gets tacky after a few wraps and becomes increasingly difficult to apply. If you are working on a rod that has 3 or 4 sections, coat no more than 1 section at a time.

If you use a rubber winding check be sure to coat it as well to prevent cracking and peeling.

Note: If you decide on a hook and ring winding check you will need to secure the ring with Scotch tape on one side and finish the *opposite* side. Wait for the epoxy to set and the finish to harden for 24 hours. Move the ring to the finished side, secure it with Scotch tape then finish the *opposite* side.

You have spent a lot of time building the rod to this stage. Since you are almost done, take time to do the job right!

Place the section you have just finished coating into the notches you cut into the empty box mentioned at the start of this Chapter.

Now it is time to sit and care for your creation! Start by making sure the guides are pointing down. The epoxy will sag soon. Turn the rod 180 degrees with the guides pointing upward. As soon as the epoxy sags turn the rod 180 degrees again. How often you need to turn the rod is unpredictable. The temperature of the epoxy, the time of year and the humidity, all influence the rate at which the epoxy sets. That is why I like to allocate about 2 hours for this process. Repeat this turning process for an hour to an hour and a half. Finally, make sure the guides are pointing down, then you can walk away. The epoxy should not move any more. All you need to do is allow the epoxy to set and dry. I like to let the rod set for 48 hours before its inauguration.

If you try to coat the whole rod, or even an entire section of a 2 piece rod, you will be frustrated because the epoxy gets too tacky and difficult to apply. Take the time to do the job right!

Buena suerte!

CHAPTER 16

FLY ROD CONSTRUCTION

I n this chapter I want to discuss, in general terms, methods used in preparing graphite for fly rods. I will approach the discussion in general terms for several reasons which, I hope, are apparent. Fly rod manufacturers are not inclined to divulge much information about their processes. Surely it is clear that this is privileged information and, as such, needs to be guarded carefully.

I give a resounding muchas gracias to Tom Dorsey of Thomas & Thomas who graciously opened his doors to me. Oren Clark gave generously of his time to explain things I had wanted to know for years but could not find anyone who was willing to share and let me "see for myself" that which I could only surmise. Tom Moran gave me insight into bamboo rod making and for his contribution I am equally grateful.

Oren made sure I had the opportunity to prepare a blank during my visit.

Photographs in this chapter were taken by the author.

The following discussions will include information about:

1. Graphite
2. Designs
3. Mandrels
4. Rolling the Graphite onto the Mandrel
5. Wrapping the Outside of the Shaft
6. Curing the Blank
7. Removing the Mandrel from the Shaft
8. Preparing the Blank

1. Graphite

Graphite is made by OEM's (Original Equipment Manufacturers) of which there are several. The rod maker creates a specification for a "cloth"; thickness, modulus of elasticity, scrim, adhesives, etc. The OEM is responsible for meeting the "spec." The exact modulus of elasticity is expressed as units, PSI and is a measure of stiffness of the material per specific volume increment.

Graphite is produced as a long, thin, continuous strand and is laid down on a substrate so that each fiber is parallel to adjacent fibers. The substrate is called "scrim." Scrim resembles window screen in composition; it is composed of longitudinal and transverse fibers. Scrim may be made of fiberglass, fiberglass and graphite or of graphite. Scrim provides hoop strength which resists crushing. Also in the matrix, thermo-set resin has been impregnated to solidify all components during the curing cycle. In recent years manufacturers use graphite scrim to provide additional hoop strength.

Graphite for the production of rods comes in rolls 1 foot or 2 feet in width and is, of course, black. Each roll can be from 200 to 1000 feet in length.

Use of a micrometer to "mike" the graphite on arrival is required to ensure the OEM has met the spec. Tolerances of 0.0001 of an inch are preferred. More critical examinations include "fiber volume analysis" which measures the precise relative quantities of resin and graphite present in a given volume unit of the cloth. The graphite is coated with resins. Since the resins can evaporate and dry the graphite is stored at temperatures below freezing. Drying can lead to cracking so the graphite needs to be properly managed before use. When needed the material is allowed to warm to room temperature and scheduled for use.

2. Designs

When the cloth is ready it is cut into tip and butt sections of proper length.

Cutting the cloth to length.

Cutting with the template.

A template is laid onto the graphite and the desired shape is cut.

As many pieces are cut as the cloth will yield.

The shape of the cut, design of the mandrel, wall thickness, slope of the mandrel and the modulus of elasticity determine the action of the rod: slow, medium or fast action.

The desired cut.

One side of the cloth is graphite, the other scrim. The manufacturer decides which side is to be attached to the mandrel. The other side is a paper backing which prevents the cloth from sticking to itself while it is still on the spool. The paper backing is removed after the cloth has been attached to the mandrel.

3. Mandrels

As a rule mandrels are made of hardened steel and coated with chrome or equivalent material to ensure longevity.

Mandrels can, and will be, used many times during their working life. As with all things nothing lasts forever and so repeated use ultimately leads to the replacement and purchase of new ones. Mandrels last about 5 years. Also, as newer materials evolve, newer mandrels must be designed and built to harmonize with the new materials. Development of newer materials falls under the purview of SAMPE (the Society for the Advancement of Materials and Processes Engineering). It is likely that materials development will lead to a fiber that will be to graphite as graphite was to fiberglass.

There are separate mandrels for each tip and butt section. The length of rod, action and line it is intended to cast will dictate the appropriate mandrel to be used. Each mandrel has 2 notches cut into its butt end.

Oren at the mandrels.

Mandrels will, of course, taper down from a larger diameter to a smaller one from the butt end to the tip end, respectively. The slope of the taper can and will vary depending on properties the maker desires the finished rod to have. Specific details about the tapers represents carefully guarded information and it is hoped that readers understand the need for protection of this information.

I have heard and spoken with some individuals about multiple tapered mandrels. While I have heard explanations about these mandrels the explanations have been less than clear. Their functionality and practicality escapes me. I would suppose that multiple tapered mandrels are considerably more expensive to manufacture than those without multiple tapers. I also cannot "see" a rod's action enhanced to a degree that would justify the additional cost to produce such mandrels. Even if multiple tapered mandrels are not expensive to produce I cannot see a significant enhancement over mandrels whose slopes are uniform.

Very close tolerances of the mandrels are necessary. The mandrel is so closely integrated to the quality and functionality of the finished rod that mandrels of low quality are not only undesirable but inexcusable.

4. Rolling the Graphite onto the Mandrel

Prior to rolling, the mandrel is prepared to accept the graphite. Each mandrel is inspected for cleanliness. The surface must be clean and free of debris from its previous use. After the mandrel is ready two agents are applied. One is a "parting" agent; the other an adhesive. The parting agent is used to facilitate separation of the mandrel from the blank after "curing." The second agent assures adhesion of the graphite to the mandrel.

The mandrel is laid in a grooved bed to prevent disorientation. The rod maker decides whether to lay the scrim side or the cloth side to the mandrel. A heat source may be used to encourage adhesives in the graphite to bond with adhesives on the mandrel.

Rolling begins when the graphite shape is attached to the mandrel at a specific location. This specific location is necessary to ensure consistency between blanks. The precise location is determined by caliper or micrometer. The edge that runs parallel to the mandrel is used. This is done to ensure proper orientation of the fibers. Once the entire length of graphite has made contact with the mandrel a careful inspection is made of the contact and the paper backing is removed. This careful alignment takes advantage of the remarkable properties of graphite; its ability to flex, its tensile strength, its modulus of elasticity and its lightness of weight.

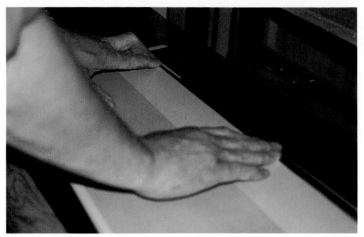

Attaching the cloth to the mandrel.

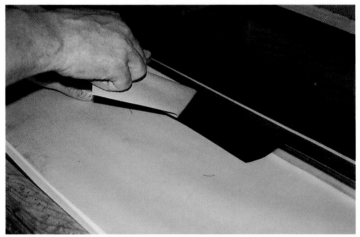

Removing the paper from the cloth.

The mandrel with its graphite design partially attached is now taken to the rolling table.

Oren at the rolling table.

The bottom half of the rolling table moves forward and rearward relative to the operator. The top half of the table has a platen. The platen rotates on an axis located

about half its length. The operator will rotate the platen so that the edge facing him is parallel to the table. The mandrel is now positioned beneath the platen in front of the operator. When ready, the operator presses 2 switches simultaneously to activate the table. The platen moves down and presses against the mandrel. The lower half of the table moves away from the operator and the graphite is rolled onto the mandrel. The platen rotates slightly on its axis during the roll. This rotation allows the platen to compensate for the difference in diameter between the butt end and tip end of the mandrel. The rotation also ensures uniform pressure from the butt to the tip end.

When the cycle is complete the table opens. The lower half of the bed recedes to its original position and the upper platen raises to its original position with a slight turn due to its rotation during the "roll."

A "pull" wrap is applied at the bottom of the butt end of the blank. Its function will be explained in the section on Removing the Mandrel from the Shaft.

5. Wrapping the Outside of the Shaft

Once the graphite has been rolled it is necessary to hold everything in place to keep the graphite from unfurling. This is done by applying an external wrap of a very narrow cellophane material. The wrapping ensures uniform compaction of the laminates and retains the impregnated resins during the "gel period" of the curing cycle where the resins migrate to the outermost part of the blank.

For this process a machine is used. The machine wraps a cellophane material around the outside of the graphite. The cellophane is wrapped onto the graphite so that there is a slight angle and overlap on the wrap. The angle is there to guide the wrap from its butt end to its tip end. The cellophane overlaps itself slightly. This overlap ensures uniformity of the wrap and that nothing is left unwrapped.

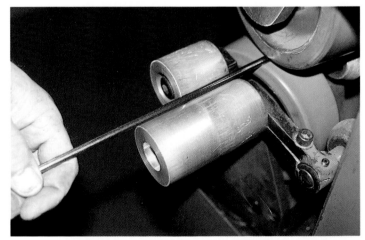

Wrapping cellophane over the shaft.

6. Curing the Blank

If you recall, the butt end of the mandrel has 2 notches cut into it. These notches are guided onto tracks in a large metal frame. The tracks are mounted at the top of the frame. An appropriate number of mandrels constituting a batch are mounted onto the frame. The mandrels are mounted vertically.

Oren at the frame.

The frame is rolled into the oven and the air-tight door is closed.

Oren at the oven.

The curing oven is brought to temperature in stages. When the proper temperature is reached convection heat is applied to ensure uniformity of temperature in the oven. Maintaining the temperature for a correct length of time is required and carefully monitored. The frame holding the blanks is now rolled into the oven. During the curing process adhesives in the graphite spread uniformly along the mandrel and create permanent bonding.

After correct aging the oven is turned off and careful cooling of the blanks begins. Culmination of the process is reached when the oven door is opened, the frame is removed and the blanks allowed to cool to room temperature.

7. Removing the Mandrel from the Shaft

Once materials have cooled, removal of the mandrel from the blank follows. This is done by placing a clamp against the "pull" wrap mentioned in Section 4; Rolling the Graphite onto the Mandrel. Another clamp is attached to the notches at the butt end of the mandrel. Once both points are secured opposing pressures are applied. The pressure is rapid and energetic. A loud, audible sound is produced at the moment when the mandrel separates from the blank.

Separation of mandrel from the blank.

Each blank is inspected for straightness and culled as necessary. Culled blanks are discarded. Accepted blanks move on to the next stage.

8. Preparing the Blank

Blanks passing inspection will now have the cellophane removed from the surface.

Scott manually removing the cellophane.

"Ridges" will be present after removal of the cellophane from the blank. Removal of ridges is done by high speed and carefully controlled sanding.

Sanding off ridges from the blank.

Following the sanding process the shafts are once again inspected to assure quality control.

At this stage decisions are made about:
    a. Leaving the surface with a matte finish.
    b. Coating and polishing the surface to a glossy finish.
    c. Adding coloring agents to the material.

Once these decisions have been made the blank is now ready for trimming, attaching the reel seat, tip top, installation of a handle, wrapping of the guides and finishing.

CHAPTER 17

ROD MATERIALS LIST

This list is to help simplify what you need for the rod.

A complete materials list, with details, is provided in Chapter 18.

1. Graphite blank of *your* choice.
2. Tip Top.
3. All metal or components reel seat with wood or cork insert of your choice.
4. Finished handle or cork rings.
5. Winding check.
6. Hook Keeper.
7. Stripping guide(s).
8. Snake guides.
9. Size A rod wrapping thread in colour(s) of your choice.
10. Thread Sealer (Read Chapter 18, Item 10 to help you decide).
11. Rod Varnish (Read Chapter 18, Item 11, Part 1 to help you decide).

Flex-Coat Epoxy (Read Chapter 18, Item 11, Part 2 to help you decide).

COMPLETE MATERIALS LIST

1. **Blank - Chapter 2.**

   The graphite blank of *your* choice.
   Refer to Chapter 2 for address and phone information about manufacturers whose blanks I use.

2. **Tip Top - Chapter 5.**

   Sizes start at about a 4 then go to 4 1/2, 5, 5 1/2, etc. You will need to select the one best fitted to your blank. Select one that slides onto the tip without friction but is not loose. I use tip tops with large loops from Pacific Bay. They also make tip tops with the smaller, traditional sized loops.

   Pacific Bay Fishing Tackle, Inc.
   540 South Jefferson Street
   Placentia, CA 92670
   714 524 1778
   1 800 272 2229 (Help Line)

3. **Reel Seat - Chapter 6.**

   Metallic reel seats are usually the least expensive. Nickel silver, while highly attractive, tarnishes readily and requires care to keep it looking new.
   Reel seats with metal components and inserts are my preference because I feel they are the most practical. With components you have the freedom to choose cork or wood inserts. I do not recommend cork because I do not consider cork to be a practical material but that is for you to decide. I much prefer wood inserts. I select my wood and have it turned to fit the components I use. As a result, my inserts have unique grain and character to them.

   I order reel seat components from:

   Glenn Struble Manufacturing
   1382 Duke Avenue
   P O Box 1370
   Sutherlin, OR 97479
   503 459 1353

4. **Handle - Chapter 10.**
   Finished Handle

   Finished handles are available in many stores or are available through mail order. You may want to order the handle at the same time you are placing an order for a blank. If you are building a rod for the first time I would suggest you consider a finished handle. I do not use finished handles but I do not hesitate recommending those made by Glenn Struble Manufacturing. See Item 3 of this chapter for address and phone information. I recommend Rod Builders Epoxy Glue available from Flex Coat.

   Flex Coat Co., Inc.
   P O Box 190
   Driftwood, TX 78619
   512 858 7742

   Cork Rings

   Order 20 to 30 rings and select 14 or 15 of the best ones for your rod. I use 13 to 14 rings on rods 7 to 8 feet in length and seldom use less. I find longer handles are more accommodating than smaller ones, irrespective of the size of a person's hand. I use 14 rings on rods 9 feet in length. If my client wants a fighting butt I use 15 rings to accommodate a reverse half Wells or full Wells handle. On fly rods for salt water I use 16, 17 or 18 rings as the line weight goes up and I will also add a forehandle of 8 to 10 rings. I locate the forehandle about 8 inches ahead of the first handle. I use this handle to relieve pressure from the dominant hand and arm; *never for fighting purposes*. Anyone using the forehandle to fight a fish runs the very high risk of breaking the rod at that point since the hand has become a fulcrum and the characteristics of the rod, painstakingly designed by the manufacturer, are severely compromised.

5. **Winding Check - Chapter 11.**

   Rubber winding check
   Rubber winding checks are functional and easy to mount. I prefer the metallic winding check because I find it harmonious with the reel seat components I use. Often, however, you will not find one that fits quite right. In almost all cases I choose a winding check that is smaller in diameter than what I need. It then becomes necessary to ream out the inside, very

slowly and carefully, to ensure proper fit. If you decide to use a metal winding check please take your time in reaming it so you do not make the hole any larger than is prudent. You are striving for a smooth, snug fit. I use the winding checks made by Struble Manufacturing. See Item 3 of this chapter for address and phone information.

6. **Hook Keeper - Chapters 3 and 12.**

One has a simple inverted U shape and this is the one I use although I do not use hook keepers on rods I build for myself. Rods for clients receive hook keepers made by Pacific Bay. See Item 2 of this chapter for address and phone information. The second has an O ring that fits into an inverted U shaped foot. When wrapped onto the rod the ring usually lays along the blank and is free to swing. The third one I have found only on Fenwick rods. I do not know of a source.

7. **Stripping Guide(s) - Chapters 9 and 12.**

Stripping guides with ceramic inserts are my first choice because they will not groove. I use the largest Pacific Bay guides the eye or client can endure. See Item 2 of this chapter for address and phone information.

8. **Snake Guides - Chapters 3, 9 and 12.**

Although I use Pacific Bay guides and they are already ground, I find it necessary to touch them up slightly. I use guides larger than anyone else. I have had discussions with two well-known personalities in fly fishing about this and have found they agree with my view. The smallest snake guide I use is number 2. I proceed to 3, 4, 5 and 6. I contend that larger guides reduce friction, static electricity and allow for smoother casts. This can also contribute to longer casts with less energy expended. There is also less clogging of guides in cold weather. I use Pacific Bay snake guides. See Item 2 of this chapter for address and phone information.

9. **Thread - Chapters 9 and 12.**

Size A - 1 small spool is enough for several rods; Gudebrod has a generous selection of colors and is available in many stores.

10. **Thread Sealer - Chapter 14.**

I use Color Preserver and Thread Sealer from Flex Coat and have been using it for years. Some argue against the use of thread sealer. As long as you are aware of the consequences you should do as you wish. If you use thread sealer it preserves the colour of the thread after the sealer dries. If you do not use thread sealer, whatever you use, whether varnish or epoxy, will absorb into the thread and changes its color characteristics. Since I always use a two color thread wrap I want a distinct color differentiation between the 2 threads; thread sealer gives me that differentiation. It also makes an excellent base for

the final coat of epoxy. See Item 4 of this chapter for address and phone information.

11. **Rod Varnish**

While I do not use it I am listing it here. You may want to try varnish. Remember, you will influence the color of the thread with the use of varnish. The varnish will readily absorb into the thread. After the thread dries it will no longer have the same coloration as it did on the spool. If you are refinishing an Orvis rod or building from an Orvis kit you may be using the brown thread used on Orvis rods. If so you will notice that the light brown thread takes on the distinctive deep brown color you see on Orvis rods after 1 coat of varnish. If you go this route please give it a second coat of varnish. This second coat will lay a good base. You may then proceed with a coat of epoxy for the finish.

Epoxy - Chapter 15.

I use High Build Polymer Rod Wrapping Finish from Flex Coat and have been using it for years. I have experimented with some of the newer epoxies, especially the thinner ones and do not care for them. The small package is enough to finish quite a few rods. The package may or may not include syringes for accurate measurement. You may encounter difficulties in finding syringes. See Item 4 of this chapter for address and phone information.

12. **Rattail file - Chapter 6.**

You will need one whether you use a finished handle or cork rings. Strive for a relatively tight fit; loose is not good. If there are points where the cork does not fit tightly against the blank, the rod may "squeak" during casting.

13. **Flat Mill bastard file - Chapter 3.**

To shape the stripping guides, snake guides and hook keeper.

14. **Scissors - Chapter 9 and 12.**

To cut thread use very sharp scissors. A second pair for coarser work such as cutting masking tape, etc, is desirable.

15. **Thompson Rod Wrapping Tool - Chapter 7.**

This is a relatively inexpensive *option*. I do not have information about where to find this tool.

16. **Whip Finishing Tool - Chapter 9 & 12.**
A loop made from monofilament fishing line will work; try 8, 10 and 12 pound test. A much better whip finisher can be made by going to a music store and buying 0.010 or 0.011 guitar wire. Cut a section of wire about 6 to 10 inches long; fold in half to form a loop. Cut a section of 1/4 inch dowel to about 1 1/2 inches in length. Drill a small hole into the dowel. Insert the loose ends of the wire loop into the hole and epoxy in place. Simple and it works.

17. **Brushes - Chapter 15.**

Available from Flex Coat. Use these to apply the thread sealer if you decide to use it. See Item 4 of this chapter for address and phone information.

18. **Lacquer Thinner**

If you use varnish. Thin only as necessary. Use it to clean the brush you use for the varnish.

19. **3/4 inch Masking Tape**

The rod builder's friend.

20. **5 Minute Epoxy - Chapters 6 and 10.**

For setting the reel seat in place and/or assembly of a components reel seat; work thoughtfully but without delay. Available at most hardware, variety, convenience or grocery stores.

21. **Slow Setting Epoxy - Chapter 10.**

Use this if you are going to use cork rings to shape your own handle. Here, again, I use Rod Builders' Epoxy Glue from Flex Coat. See Item 4 of this chapter for address and phone information.

22. **Sandpaper - Chapter 10.**

If you have decided to shape your own handle, do your turning at high speeds; up to 4000 RPM is acceptable. You need high speed to remove soft material like cork with 60, 100 and 220 grit sandpaper; 1 or 2 inches in width; 5 to 6 inches in length. Start with 60 in the very early stage of shaping the handle to remove cork. Move to 100 as the desired shape is reached and keep working with this grit until you get *almost* the shape you want. Move to 220 to touch-up. Without doubt you will need to fill-in holes in the cork. Cork of exceptional quality has been unavailable for years. Stay with it to completion. At this point you want to "polish" rather than remove material.

23. **Birch/Fir Putty - Chapter 10.**

To fill holes in the cork. Work the putty well into each hole. Use the 220 grit sandpaper to smooth out bumps and remove *only enough* to achieve desired results.

24. **High Speed Drill - Chapter 10.**

Only if you are going to shape your own handle. If you have access to a lathe, use it.

25. **Reaming Tool - Chapter 11.**

To ream out metal winding check.

26. **Matches, Cigarette Lighter or Alcohol Lamp - Chapter 13.**

To "fight the fuzzies."

27. **Vice - Chapter 10.**

To hold inverted high speed drill. A lathe is much better if you have access to one.

28. **L Brackets - Chapter 10.**

To make a stand for holding the free end of the handle when shaping your own handle.

29. **Furring Strip - Chapter 10.**

Used in conjunction with the L brackets to make a stand for holding the free end of the handle when shaping your own handle.

30. **Mixing Bowl - Chapter 15.**

Just about any kind of small, shallow dish will do. Plastic is o.k. and it can be discarded. These are available from Flex Coat. See Item 4, this chapter for address and phone information. I use a mixing bowl available from Jack Perry. Jack has good, solid, practical ideas for tools, both for rod building and fly tying. The mixing bowl, with care, will last a lifetime.

Perry Design
7401 Zircon Drive, SW
Tacoma, WA 98498
206 582 1555

31. **Knitting Needle - Chapter 15.**

To apply the finishing coat of epoxy.

32. **Sewing Needle - Chapter 5.**

To apply epoxy to the inside of the tip top and to the tip of the tip section when installing the tip top.

33. **Alcohol and/or Acetone - Chapter 13.**

To clean the surface in case of a need to re-wrap.

34. **Butane Type Cigarette Lighter - Chapter 13.**

To eliminate "fuzzies".

35. **Thin Bladed Knife with a *Dull* Blade - Chapter 13.**

To remove a wrap should the need arise.

36. **Empty Cardboard Box - Chapter 15.**

To use for wrapping the rod and to turn the rod during the final stage of completion.

37. **Two Syringes - Chapter 15.**

For accurately measuring equal amounts of resin and hardener to apply epoxy. They are available from Flex Coat. See Item 4, this chapter, for address and phone information.

38. **1/4 inch Dowel**

To make a whip finishing tool. Refer to Item 16 of this chapter.

39. **Smooth Elastic**

Narrow, smooth elastic as used for women's underwear. Cut a section about 10 inches long and sew together to form a circle. Use in conjunction with Items 28 and 29 of this chapter to hold down the free end of the reel seat if shaping your own handle using an inverted drill setup. Further, if using this setup wrap a strip of paper over the insert and secure it in place with masking tape. This will prevent the elastic from scoring the surface of the cork or wood insert. If you use a lathe you will not need this item.

CHAPTER 19

GUIDE SPACINGS

Before deciding to use the guide spacings given here *I strongly recommend* you use the spacings provided by the manufacturer of the blank you will be using to build your rod.

I have found all of them willing to provide this information. They have a vested interest in what you are doing and want to help you do the best possible job you can.

A store in your area may have a finished rod from the manufacturer whose blank you have chosen. Visit the store and ask for the spacings or take them directly from a finished rod that matches the one you are going to build. This is a safe decision and one you should follow.

All measurements are from the tip end of the blank for a 1 piece rod.

For a blank with multiple sections measure from the tip end of each section unless you are told to put the various sections together before measuring.

5 ft - 1 piece
5-1/4" • 11-1/4" • 19" • 27" • 35"

6 1/2 ft - 2 sections
Tip: 4-1/2" • 11" • 18-1/4" • 26" • 34-5/8"
Butt: 2-5/8" • 13"

6-1/2 ft - 3 sections
Tip: 4-3/4" • 10-1/4" • 16-1/4" • 23"
Middle: 2-1/2" • 7-1/2" • 13-3/4" • 20-1/4"
Butt: 3"

7 ft - 2 sections
Tip: 4-1/2" • 10-1/4" • 16-1/2" • 23" • 30-1/4"
• 37-1/2"
Butt: 4-1/4" • 13-1/2"

7-1/2 ft - 2 sections
Tip: 4-3/8" • 9-3/4" • 15-5/8" • 21-5/8" • 28"
• 34- 7/8" • 43-1/2"
Butt: 5" -•16-1/2"

8 ft - 2 sections
Tip: 5-1/8" • 10-1/2" • 16" • 22" • 28-1/4"
• 35-1/2" • 44"
Butt: 7-7/8" • 19-1/4"

8-1/2 ft - 2 sections
Tip: 4-7/8" • 10-7/8" • 17-5/8" • 24-1/2"
• 31-1/2" • 38-3/4" • 46-5/8"
Butt: 3-7/8" • 12-1/8" •21-1/2"

9 ft - 2 sections
Tip: 5" • 10-1/2" • 16-1/4" • 22-3/8" • 28-1/2"
• 35" • 41-3/4" • 49"
Butt: 4" • 12-5/8" • 23-1/2"

9-1/2 ft - 2 sections
Tip: 5" • 10-3/8" • 16-3/8" • 22-1/2" • 29"
• 35-3/4" • 43" • 51"
Butt: 4" -•12-1/2" • 22-1/2"

10 ft - 2 sections
Tip: 4-1/2" • 9-3/8" • 14-1/2" • 19-3/4"
• 26-3/4" • 33-1/2" • 40-1/2" • 48" • 55-1/2"
Butt: 6" • 14-1/2" • 24-1/4"

10 ft - 3 sections
Tip: 5" • 10-1/2" • 16" •22-1/4" • 28-3/4" • 35-1/4"
Middle: 3-1/4" • 10-1/2" • 18-1/4" •26-1/4" • 34-3/4"
Butt: 7-1/4"

10-1/2 ft - 3 sections
Tip: 5-1/4" • 10-3/4" • 16-3/4" • 23-1/2"
• 30-1/4" • 37"
Middle: 5-1/4" • 11-3/4" • 19-3/4" • 27-1/4"
•36-1/4"
Butt: 5-1/2" • 15-1/4

LEARN MORE ABOUT FLY FISHING AND FLY TYING WITH THESE BOOKS

If you are unable to find the books shown below at your local book store
or fly shop you can order direct from the publisher below.

Flies: The Best One Thousand
Randy Stetzer
$24.95

Fly Tying Made Clear and Simple
Skip Morris
$19.95 (HB: $29.95)

The Art of Tying the Dry Fly
Skip Morris
$29.95 (HB:$39.95)

Curtis Creek Manifesto
Sheridan Anderson
$7.95

American Fly Tying Manual
Dave Hughes
$9.95

The Art and Science of Fly Fishing
Lenox Dick
$19.95

Western Hatches
Dave Hughes, Rick Hafele
$24.95

Lake Fishing with a Fly
Ron Cordes, Randall Kaufmann
$26.95

Advanced Fly Fishing for Steelhead
Deke Meyer
$24.95

Fly Patterns of Alaska
Alaska Flyfishers
$19.95

Fly Tying & Fishing for Panfish and Bass
Tom Keith
$19.95

Float Tube Fly Fishing
Deke Meyer
$11.95